CONTENTS

INTRODUCTION

Imagine a job where every day brings new challenges, the environment is intense, and the responsibility for maintaining order and safety of those within the wall rests on your shoulders. This is the daily reality for lead correctional officers. These individuals' step into high-stress environments where the balance between safety and chaos is delicate and ever-shifting. Yet, day after day, they return, committed to their roles, managing the complexities of prison life and ensuring the well-being of incarcerated individuals and staff. What drives these officers to stay dedicated in such a demanding profession?

This book seeks to answer that question, offering an in-depth exploration into the motivations and experiences of lead correctional officers within a specific Midwest State Department of Corrections. Often overlooked, their leadership is pivotal to the functioning of the prison system, and their stories offer valuable insights into the personal and professional challenges they face. What keeps them going? What fuels their commitment, and how do they navigate the constant pressures of such a high-stakes role?

By delving into their world, we gain a deeper understanding of the forces that shape their professional lives. Beyond the day-to-day management of prison facilities, lead correctional officers must contend with complex interpersonal dynamics, institutional challenges, and the personal resilience required to withstand the emotional toll of their work. This study sheds light on the officers' individual experiences and how these insights can inform better support systems and training programs, ultimately contributing to a more effective and humane correctional system.

Through the pages of this book, we invite you to step into the heart of correctional work, where dedication meets resilience and the quest for justice unfolds within the corridors of state prisons.

CHAPTER 1: THE FOCUS OF OUR STUDY

Imagine stepping into a role where every day brings new challenges, where the responsibility for safety, order, and rehabilitation within a state correctional facility falls on your shoulders. This is the daily reality for lead correctional officers —those identified as Corrections Officer 3 (sergeant)—within a state in the Midwest region of the United States. These officers are vital to the functioning of the state's Department of Corrections, serving as leaders who manage both the staff and the incarcerated individuals under their care. Yet despite their critical roles, they remain underrepresented and understudied in academic research.

This book aims to fill that gap by investigating what motivates these officers to continue working in such a challenging and demanding environment. To provide context, consider the scope of the Minnesota Department of Corrections. According to the Office of the Legislative Auditor (OLA,

2020), approximately 9,200 individuals were incarcerated across Minnesota's 11 state correctional facilities in 2020. The department employs around 3,700 staff members, including correctional officers and support personnel. These numbers reflect the complexity of maintaining order and rehabilitating incarcerated individuals within the state's prison system. Yet, beneath these figures lies a persistent issue—chronic staffing shortages, which have had a profound impact on both the incarcerated population and the officers who serve them. These statistics, drawn from pre-COVID-19 data, likely mask even deeper challenges brought on by the pandemic.

One of the most pressing concerns identified by the OLA report (2020) is the high turnover rate among correctional officers. This challenge has contributed to staffing levels consistently falling below budgeted allocations, occasionally resulting in the suspension of vital services, including therapy, educational programs, and recreational activities within the prisons. The fluctuations in staffing place additional stress on both the system and its workforce. For example, one facility experienced an average annual turnover rate of 11.2% from 2014 to 2018, which jumped to 17.7% in 2019. Another facility saw a turnover rate of 15.1% during that same year, up from a previous five-year average of 9.9% (OLA, 2020).

This turnover impacts not only on operations but also on the well-being of those tasked with running these facilities. While some officers transition to other roles within the Department of Corrections, others leave the profession entirely, exacerbating the staffing shortages and heightening the workload for those who remain. Recognizing these challenges, the Minnesota Department of Corrections emphasized in its 2021 Performance Report (MNDOC, 2021) the critical role of its staff in maintaining core operations and ensuring the safety of incarcerated individuals. The department also highlighted its commitment to fostering a supportive work environment for its 4,340 employees and its collaboration with labor unions to improve working conditions.

The toll on corrections officers is well-documented in the literature. Studies have shown that constant exposure to violence, managing volatile situations, and maintaining authority can take a significant psychological and physical toll on officers (Shepherd et al., 2018; Trounson & Pfeifer, 2017; Vickovic & Morrow, 2020). Research suggests that these stressors can lead to burnout, emotional exhaustion, and health problems, all of which undermine job satisfaction and retention (Isenhardt & Hostettler, 2020; Evers et al., 2020). In addition to operational challenges, correctional officers must navigate complex emotional landscapes. Their daily interactions with incarcerated individuals, the families of incarcerated individuals, and the public create emotional strain, further contributing to burnout (Ricciardelli, 2017). Given these pressures, it is no surprise that corrections officers report elevated levels of job dissatisfaction, a key factor in their decisions to leave the profession.

While much of the existing research focuses on the negative

aspects of corrections work, there is also evidence suggesting that self-efficacy and motivation can serve as protective factors. Studies in related service professions, such as nursing, have found that individuals with elevated levels of self-efficacy, those who believe in their ability to handle difficult situations —are less likely to experience burnout (Fida et al., 2018). This aligns with Bandura's social cognitive theory, which emphasizes the importance of individuals' belief in their ability to succeed (Bandura, 2001). Understanding what motivates lead correctional officers to remain in their roles is crucial for improving recruitment, retention, and training strategies in corrections systems.

This study, therefore, aims to provide a deeper understanding of the subjective experiences and motivations of lead correctional officers, particularly those in Minnesota's Department of Corrections. Through interviews and data collection, this research explores the factors that keep these officers committed to their work despite the daily challenges they face. By amplifying their voices, this study seeks to offer practical insights for corrections leaders to better support their staff, ultimately enhancing the well-being of correctional officers and improving the overall functioning of state corrections systems.

In conclusion, the focus of this study is to document the experiences of lead correctional officers, shedding light on their dedication, resilience, and the factors that motivate them to stay in such a demanding profession. By doing so, this research contributes to a broader understanding of corrections work, offering practical recommendations for supporting these vital members of the criminal justice system.

CHAPTER 2: WHY THIS STUDY MATTERS

In the world of corrections, where safety, order, and rehabilitation are tightly intertwined, understanding the motivations behind why lead correctional officers remain in their positions is crucial. Throughout our research, it became evident that gaining insights into what drives these officers could have far-reaching implications for multiple stakeholders. For corrections departments, understanding these factors could inform more effective training, mentoring programs, and recruitment processes.

For the officers themselves, uncovering the elements that contribute to their job satisfaction can lead to improvements in working conditions, support systems, and overall well-being. Ultimately, this study provides a foundation for broader research into correctional staff experiences, contributing to organizational improvement and the field of psychology. Lead correctional officers, specifically those identified as Corrections Officer 3 (sergeants), play a pivotal role in maintaining daily operations within prison institutions. Their work demands direct interaction with incarcerated individuals under challenging and unpredictable conditions. Yet, despite their critical role, their experiences and challenges still need to be explored in academic literature. This study seeks to address that gap, comprehensively examining what motivates them to stay committed to such a demanding profession.

The Importance of Correctional Officers' Well-being

Several studies have emphasized the psychological and physical toll that corrections officers endure. Research consistently highlights how the stressors inherent in the job—such as witnessing violence, managing volatile situations, and navigating complex relationships with incarcerated individuals—can significantly impact their mental health and job satisfaction (Shepherd et al., 2018; Trounson & Pfeifer, 2017; Vickovic & Morrow, 2020).

The continuous emotional strain can lead to burnout, decreased job satisfaction, and adverse health outcomes

(Isenhardt & Hostettler, 2020; Munger et al., 2015).

Burnout among correctional officers is not just a personal issue; it affects the entire correctional system. The well-being of correctional officers influences their performance, impacting on the incarcerated individuals they supervise and the overall environment of correctional institutions. Addressing the root causes of stress and dissatisfaction is essential for maintaining a healthy, effective workforce.

Understanding the Ripple Effect

One of the key findings from the literature is the ripple effect that officers' job satisfaction (or dissatisfaction) has on their colleagues, incarcerated individuals, and the institution as a whole. When correctional officers are supported and feel satisfied in their roles, the quality of their interactions with incarcerated individuals improves, which can enhance rehabilitation outcomes (Moon & Maxwell, 2004). On the other hand, high stress and low morale among officers can exacerbate tensions within the prison, making it more difficult to maintain order and leading to higher turnover rates, further destabilizing the system.

Interventions That Work

A growing body of research highlights effective interventions for improving the well-being of correctional officers. Evers et al. (2020) explored various interventions to enhance officers' mental health, job satisfaction, and resilience. Techniques such as cognitive-behavioral therapy, mindfulness-based approaches, resilience training, and social support programs have all been found to make a measurable difference. These findings suggest that the corrections departments could improve officer retention and job satisfaction by investing in these support programs.

Similarly, Trounson and Pfeifer (2017) examined the coping mechanisms officers use when facing adversity, noting that negative strategies—such as emotional venting or suppression—can heighten stress levels and strain workplace relationships. Their work emphasizes the need for targeted interventions to address these harmful coping strategies and promote a healthier work environment.

The Role of Motivation

Motivation is a key subject throughout literature, as it significantly influences job performance and satisfaction. Van den Broeck et al. (2021) conducted research using self-determination theory to examine the role of motivation in high-stress professions like corrections. Their findings suggest that intrinsic motivation—when individuals find meaning and purpose in their work—is intricately linked to favorable work-related outcomes, such as enhanced job performance and greater satisfaction. Understanding the motivational drivers of correctional officers is crucial for developing policies and practices that encourage long-term retention and high job satisfaction.

For corrections departments, fostering intrinsic motivation may involve giving officers more autonomy, providing opportunities for professional development, and creating a sense of purpose in their work. These organizational changes could address some of the root causes of burnout and turnover.

Mental Health and Resilience in Corrections

Burnout and mental health challenges are common in the field of corrections. Klinoff et al. (2018) explored the relationship between resilience and burnout among correctional officers, finding that those with higher resilience levels tend to experience lower rates of burnout. Resilience, bolstered by social support from supervisors and colleagues, is a protective factor that mitigates the effects of job stress. This research suggests that corrections departments could reduce burnout by building a more supportive workplace culture.

Studies by Rhineberger-Dunn and Mack (2019) also highlight the importance of organizational factors, such as job control and fairness, in reducing stress and promoting job satisfaction. When officers feel they have control over their work and perceive the institution as just and fair, their stress levels decrease, and job satisfaction improves.

Gender Differences in Corrections

It's important to note that the experiences of correctional officers are not homogenous. Lambert et al. (2022) found significant gender differences in how correctional officers experience stress. Female officers reported higher levels of stress compared to their male counterparts, highlighting the need for gender-specific support systems and interventions. Additionally, Burdett et al. (2018) documented the challenges female officers face, including discrimination, stereotyping, and issues with career advancement. Addressing these gender-specific issues is critical to creating a more inclusive and supportive work environment for all officers.

The Need for Further Research

While existing research has provided valuable insights into the stressors, coping strategies, and well-being of correctional officers, there remains a notable gap in understanding the experiences of lead correctional officers. This study seeks to fill that gap by exploring the personal motivations and experiences of these officers to inform better policies and practices within corrections.

Conclusion

By understanding what motivates lead correctional officers to stay in their roles, we can better support their mental health, job satisfaction, and resilience. This research contributes to the broader field of psychology and provides practical recommendations for corrections departments to improve training, mentoring, and organizational support systems. Ultimately, this study aims to create a more resilient and effective corrections workforce, benefiting the officers and the broader prison system.

CHAPTER 3: METHODOLOGY

AND APPROACH

This chapter outlines the methodological framework employed to explore the motivations and experiences of lead correctional officers. Using a generic qualitative research design, we gathered subjective insights into the opinions, attitudes, and reflections of officers in correctional leadership positions.

Through open-ended, semi-structured interviews with eight lead correctional officers, each having 15 to 16 years of service, we identified key themes and patterns that reveal what keeps them committed to their challenging roles. This chapter details the purpose, focus, and methods used for data collection and analysis and addresses ethical considerations, participant protection, and the researcher's role.

Purpose of the Study

The primary purpose of this study was to gain an in-depth understanding of the subjective experiences of lead correctional officers and the factors that motivate them to continue their work. Correctional officers are integral to the daily functioning of prison institutions, often operating in highly stressful and unpredictable environments.

By examining the reflections of lead correctional officers, this research provides valuable insights that can benefit stakeholders in understanding officers' motivations. This knowledge has practical applications for improving training programs, mentoring, and recruitment strategies within state correctional systems. Additionally, this study contributes to the broader field of psychology and lays the groundwork for future research into the experiences of correctional staff.

Research Question

This study was guided by the following research question:

"How do lead correctional officers experience and describe their subjective reflections concerning what motivates them to maintain their employment?"

Research Design

To address the research question, a generic qualitative inquiry was chosen as the most appropriate method for exploring the subjective experiences of correctional officers. As described by Kostere and Kostere (2021), a generic qualitative approach allows researchers to focus on understanding the meaning participants attribute to a phenomenon based on their individual experiences.

This methodology emphasizes human experience, and the language participants use to describe their perceptions and feelings. The design is particularly well-suited for studies aiming to gain insights into personal reflections, beliefs, and motivations without adhering to the more rigid structures of other qualitative research approaches like phenomenology or grounded theory.

In line with qualitative inquiry, semi-structured interviews were conducted. This approach allowed for flexibility in the conversation while ensuring that key topics were covered. The open-ended nature of the questions enabled participants to share detailed descriptions of their experiences, helping to uncover rich data that revealed patterns and themes related to their motivations.

Target Population and Sample

The research population for this study consisted of lead correctional officers—specifically those identified as Correctional Officer 3 (sergeant)employed in state correctional facilities. This population was selected because of their leadership roles and direct involvement in managing incarcerated individuals and staff within the prison system. These individuals are tasked with maintaining safety and security while overseeing the enforcement of institutional rules and providing guidance to those under their leadership.

Sample

The sample consisted of eight lead correctional officers, each with an average of 15 to 16 years of experience. Participants were selected through purposeful sampling, a technique commonly used in qualitative research to ensure that participants have direct experience with the phenomenon under study. The sample size was determined based on data saturation, which occurs when no new themes or insights emerge from the data.

Inclusion Criteria

- Full-time lead correctional officers (Corrections Officer 3) working 35-40 hours per week.
- Officers who had not received disciplinary actions within the last 12 months.
- Officers are willing to share their experiences and insights regarding their motivations to maintain employment.

Exclusion Criteria

- Officers who were currently facing disciplinary actions or receiving mental health treatment for conditions such as PTSD, anxiety, depression, or substance use disorders.
- Officers are employed at the same correctional facility as the researcher to avoid conflicts of interest.

Procedures

The following procedures were followed for participant selection, data collection, and protection:

1. **Recruitment**: Recruitment letters were posted on staff bulletin boards and the Midwestern State Department of Corrections intranet. Interested participants contacted the researcher directly to express interest in the study.
2. **Screening**: Zoom interviews were conducted with potential participants to determine their eligibility. Qualified individuals were asked to sign an informed

consent form.

3. **Interviews**: Semi-structured interviews were conducted over Zoom, lasting 30 minutes to 1 hour. Interviews were recorded and transcribed for data analysis.
4. **Protection of Participants**: Each participant was assigned an alphanumeric code (P1, P2, etc.) to ensure confidentiality. Informed consent was obtained before each interview, and participants were assured of their privacy and the right to withdraw from the study at any time. All personal data was securely stored and will be destroyed after seven years in compliance with Capella University's guidelines.

Data Collection

Data collection involved in-depth, semi-structured interviews. The use of open-ended questions allowed participants to explore their thoughts and feelings flexibly, providing detailed insights into their experiences and motivations. Each interview followed a framework of guiding questions while allowing room for probing deeper into specific areas of interest.

Interview questions included:

1. What motivated you to work as a lead correctional officer?
2. What have your motivational experiences in this profession allowed you to discover about yourself?
3. What has helped facilitate the development of motivational influences in maintaining your

employment?

4. What has been your biggest challenge in maintaining your employment?

These questions and probing follow-ups helped create a comprehensive view of the participants' experiences.

Data Analysis

Once the interviews were transcribed, the data was analyzed using thematic analysis, a method well-suited for identifying patterns and themes across qualitative data. Thematic analysis followed a structured process of coding and categorizing the data, allowing for the emergence of themes related to the motivations of lead correctional officers.

Steps involved in data analysis included:

1. **Familiarization with Data**: Reading and re-reading transcripts to familiarize oneself with the content.
2. **Initial Coding**: Coding meaningful data segments line-by-line to identify recurring themes and patterns.
3. **Theme Development**: Grouping related codes into broader themes that addressed the research question.
4. **Review and Refinement**: Revisiting themes to ensure they accurately captured the data and were supported by direct quotes from participants.

The Role of the Researcher

As the primary instrument of data collection and analysis,

it was essential for the researcher to remain aware of personal biases and set them aside to maintain objectivity. Given the researcher's professional background in corrections, careful steps were taken to ensure that the researcher's experiences did not influence data collection or interpretation. Additionally, the researcher's responsibility included safeguarding participants' ethical treatment and ensuring the study's credibility and trustworthiness.

Ethical Considerations

Ethical considerations were central to the study design. Following the American Psychological Association (APA) guidelines, informed consent was obtained from all participants, and confidentiality was strictly maintained. Participants were fully informed of the study's purpose, their rights, and the limits of confidentiality. Additionally, the researcher avoided conflicts of interest, especially since the study occurred in the same field where the researcher is professionally employed.

Summary

Chapter 3 provided an overview of this study's research methodology and approach. By employing a generic qualitative research design, this study aimed to capture the subjective reflections of lead correctional officers regarding their motivations. The chapter detailed the procedures for participant selection, data collection, and data analysis, along with the ethical considerations addressed throughout the study. Chapter 4 presents the study's findings, offering a detailed exploration of the themes and insights gathered from the participants.

CHAPTER 4: KEY FINDINGS

This chapter presents the key findings from the analysis of interviews with eight lead correctional officers, each with an average of 15 to 16 years of experience.

Table 1

Participant Demographics

Participant (P)	Years in Service	Years as a Sergeant
P1	15-20	less than 5
P2	less than 10	less than 5
P3	10-15	5-10
P4	10-15	less than 5
P5	less than 10	5 years
P6	15-20	5-10
P7	20-25	10-15
P8	25-30	15-20

Note. Years worked are presented as ranges to further de-identify participants.

Using Bandura's self-efficacy theory as a guiding framework, we identified seven major themes supported by 14 patterns that highlight the factors that motivate officers to remain in their roles despite the significant challenges inherent in the correctional environment. These themes provide a nuanced understanding of the motivations that drive job retention, ranging from financial stability to interpersonal relationships and the impact of gender dynamics within the correctional system.

Table 2

Themes and Patterns

Theme	Pattern 1	Pattern 2	Pattern 3
Theme 1. Financial Stability	Pattern 1.1. Employment benefits	Pattern 1.2. Job security	
Theme 2. Work-Life Balance	Pattern 2.1. Stress and mental health	Pattern 2.2. Self-care and mental health	Pattern 2.3. Support
Theme 3. Interpersonal Relationships	Pattern 3.1. Peer relationship	Pattern 3.2. Supervisor relationship	Pattern 3.3. Family relationship
Theme 4. Supportive Environment	Pattern 4.1. Opportunity to advance	Pattern 4.2. Feelings matter	Pattern 4.3. Team
Theme 5. Autonomy	Pattern 5.1. Desire for leadership and autonomy	Pattern 5.2. Challenges and priorities	
Theme 6. Professionalism	Pattern 6.1. Self-Awareness and delegation	Pattern 6.2. Work ethic and fulfilling responsibilities	
Theme 7. Gender Dynamic in Corrections	Pattern 7.1. Decline in female staff	Pattern 7.2. Challenges of being a female staff in male-dominated environment	Pattern 7.3. Limited female representation in leadership roles

Theme 1: Financial Stability

One of the strongest motivators for the participants was financial stability. Correctional officers consistently referenced the financial benefits that come with their roles, including job security, pensions, and comprehensive health coverage.

Pattern 1.1: Employment Benefits

Participants emphasized the significance of employment benefits such as vacation time, pension plans, health insurance, and overtime pay. These benefits were seen as vital to their long-term commitment to the job.

- *P1:* "I love the amount of vacation time I get. It's a huge part of why I stay. The benefits and pension are also key."
- *P4:* "Health insurance and retirement benefits are big for me. They make a huge difference in why I stay here."

Pattern 1.2: Job Security

Job security was another crucial factor. Participants expressed reluctance to leave a stable position, especially considering their length of service and the effort it would take to start over in a new field.

- *P1:* "I have valuable experience, and I don't want to start over elsewhere."
- *P8:* "After working here so long, finding a similar job with comparable pay and benefits would be difficult."

Theme 2: Work-Life Balance

Work-life balance emerged as a critical theme, with participants emphasizing the importance of maintaining separation between the stresses of their job and their personal lives.

Pattern 2.1: Stress and Burnout

Several participants spoke of the intense emotional and physical stress they experience on the job. Burnout was a concern, and many expressed that balancing work with personal time was essential to maintaining their mental health.

- *P4:* "The stress can be overwhelming at times, but separating work from my personal life helps me cope."
- *P8:* "This job is mentally and physically exhausting, and the only way to deal with it is to have a balance between work and home."

Pattern 2.2: Self-Care and Mental Health

Participants described self-care practices as a way to mitigate stress. This included exercise, spending time with family, and engaging in hobbies that had nothing to do with work.

- *P7:* "When I come home, I need about half an hour to decompress before I can interact with my family."
- *P4:* "Physical exercise and hobbies like riding my motorcycle are what keep me grounded."

Pattern 2.3: Support Systems

Family and community support systems were also critical. Officers acknowledged the importance of understanding family members and friends who helped them manage the emotional toll of the job.

- *P4:* "Having good people to talk to and a supportive family helps me get through the tough days."

Theme 3: Interpersonal Relationships

The relationships officers had with their peers, supervisors, and families were central to their job satisfaction and motivation to stay in their roles.

Pattern 3.1: Peer Relationships

A sense of camaraderie among officers played a vital role in job satisfaction. Participants described their peers as a second family, fostering a support system that helped them endure the difficulties of the job.

- *P4:* "We're a close-knit group, and that bond helps us get through tough situations together."
- *P7:* "I really enjoy working with my peers; we look out for each other."

Pattern 3.2: Supervisor Relationships

Participants emphasized the importance of having respectful and supportive relationships with their supervisors. Mutual respect fostered a positive work environment and enhanced their motivation to continue in their roles.

- *P3:* "When you have a supervisor who respects you and reciprocates that respect, it makes a big difference in how you feel about your job."
- *P8:* "Good supervisors can make all the difference. If they support you, it makes coming to work a lot easier."

Pattern 3.3: Family Relationships

The impact of the job on family relationships was significant.

Officers spoke about the challenges of working long hours, weekends, and holidays, which sometimes led to marital strain. However, strong family support systems helped them manage these challenges.

- *P7:* "The job contributed to my divorce, but having a good family support system has helped me cope."

Theme 4: Supportive Environment

Officers valued a supportive work environment that provided opportunities for career advancement, autonomy, and teamwork. They expressed satisfaction with their contributions to the workplace and the ability to make decisions independently.

Pattern 4.1: Career Advancement Opportunities

While some officers expressed an interest in career advancement, others felt content in their current positions. They appreciated the flexibility to grow within the organization.

- *P4:* "I feel like I have a lot of opportunities for advancement if I want them, but I'm also happy where I am."

Pattern 4.2: Sense of Mattering

Many officers felt that their contributions to the workplace mattered. They found motivation in the belief that their work was meaningful and had a positive impact on others.

> · *P1:* "I feel like what I do matters. It's rewarding to know that I make a difference."

Pattern 4.3: Teamwork and Camaraderie

Teamwork was emphasized as a key factor in maintaining job satisfaction. Participants described their colleagues as family and appreciated the collaborative nature of their work.

> · *P7:* "It's a dysfunctional family at times, but it's still a family. We rely on each other every day."

Theme 5: Autonomy

Autonomy and the ability to make independent decisions were highly valued. Participants appreciated leadership roles that allowed them the freedom to manage their teams and make decisions without micromanagement.

Pattern 5.1: Desire for Leadership

Leadership roles offered opportunities for autonomy, which many officers found motivating. They enjoyed having the authority to manage their teams and make decisions independently.

- *P5:* "I like being in charge and having the freedom to make decisions that affect my team."

Pattern 5.2: Frustrations with Organizational Limitations

While autonomy was valued, some officers expressed frustration with organizational limitations, such as micromanagement and trivial issues being prioritized over more significant concerns.

- *P2:* "It's frustrating when you're micromanaged over trivial matters when there are bigger issues to deal with."

Theme 6: Professionalism

Professionalism, personal integrity, and fulfilling responsibilities were essential aspects of officers' motivation. Participants took pride in their work, viewing their roles as an opportunity to lead by example and ensure the safety and success of their teams.

Pattern 6.1: Self-Awareness and Delegation

Officers recognized the importance of understanding their strengths and weaknesses and delegating tasks when necessary to maintain professionalism.

- *P2:* "It's important to know your strengths and delegate tasks accordingly. That's part of being a good leader."

Pattern 6.2: Work Ethic and Fulfilling Responsibilities

A strong work ethic and commitment to fulfilling responsibilities were central to officers' sense of professionalism. They felt satisfaction in doing their jobs well and supporting their colleagues.

- *P4:* "I take pride in my work and feel responsible for making sure things run smoothly for my team."

Theme 7: Gender Dynamics in Corrections

The gender dynamics within correctional facilities posed unique challenges, particularly for female officers. Participants noted the decline in female staff and the limited representation of women in leadership roles.

Pattern 7.1: Decline in Female Staff

Several participants noted a decline in the number of female staff, attributing this to the challenges faced by women in a male-dominated work environment.

- *P3:* "There are fewer female officers now than when I started. It's tough for women to advance in this field."

Pattern 7.2: Challenges for Female Officers

Female officers faced additional challenges in navigating the male-dominated work environment, particularly when working with male incarcerated individuals.

- *P8:* "Being a woman in this field is tough, especially when working with male incarcerated individuals. It adds a layer of complexity to the job."

Pattern 7.3: Limited Female Representation in Leadership

Participants pointed out the limited representation of women in leadership roles, with few women reaching positions such as sergeant or lieutenant.

- *P8:* "There are very few female sergeants and even fewer women in higher leadership roles. It's a problem that needs to be addressed."

Summary

The analysis of interviews with lead correctional officers uncovered seven major themes that provide insights into the factors that motivate them to remain in their roles. These themes—financial stability, work-life balance, interpersonal relationships, a supportive environment, autonomy, professionalism, and gender dynamics—reflect the complex and multifaceted nature of job retention in the correctional field.

By understanding these factors, organizations can

implement strategies to improve job satisfaction, support systems, and opportunities for career growth, ultimately reducing turnover rates and fostering a healthier work environment for correctional officers. The findings also highlight the need for gender diversity and inclusion in leadership roles within correctional institutions.

CHAPTER 5: PRACTICAL IMPLICATIONS

The findings from this research on correctional officers' motivations to maintain their employment provide valuable insights into improving workplace conditions, policies, and support systems in correctional facilities. By understanding the key motivators—financial stability, work-life balance, interpersonal relationships, supportive environments, autonomy, professionalism, and gender dynamics—appointing authorities can create a more engaged, committed, and satisfied workforce. This chapter explores the practical implications of these findings to offer recommendations for fostering a more motivated and stable workforce.

Understanding and Enhancing

Correctional Officers' Motivators

Lead correctional officers experience various challenges and rewards that impact their decision to stay in the field. Financial stability and job security were paramount for the participants, as were the supportive relationships they fostered with peers and supervisors. Additionally, a healthy work-life balance, opportunities for professional growth, and a supportive work environment contributed to their overall job satisfaction. Correctional facilities can improve retention rates and officer well-being by addressing these factors through policy changes and strategic initiatives.

Practical Recommendations for Improvement

1. Financial Stability and Compensation Packages

Participants consistently highlighted the importance of competitive compensation and comprehensive benefits packages in motivating them to stay in their positions. Correctional facilities should prioritize offering competitive salaries, pensions, and benefits to attract and retain experienced officers. Increasing opportunities for overtime pay and including retirement incentives can further bolster financial security and job satisfaction.

2. Promoting Work-Life Balance and Mental Health

Work-life balance is essential for mitigating stress and burnout inherent in correctional work. Participants noted the significance of self-care practices and supportive resources for maintaining physical and mental well-being. Correctional facilities should implement policies that promote flexible scheduling, adequate time off, and stress-reduction programs. Additionally, investing in mental health support, including counseling services and wellness programs, can help officers manage the emotional toll of their work.

3. Fostering Positive Interpersonal Relationships

Positive relationships with peers and supervisors were key to the participants' job satisfaction. Correctional facilities can improve the quality of workplace relationships by promoting a culture of respect, open communication, and mutual support. This can be achieved through team-building exercises, supervisor leadership development programs, and mentoring programs that encourage collaboration and camaraderie among officers. Strong interpersonal relationships can enhance job satisfaction and lead to better job performance.

4. Creating a Supportive Environment

Lead correctional officers expressed the importance of

a supportive work environment that values autonomy, professionalism, and opportunities for career advancement. Correctional facilities should ensure officers have access to clear promotion and professional development pathways. Regular training, mentorship opportunities, and leadership programs can empower officers to take on greater responsibilities and feel accomplished in their roles. Additionally, promoting autonomy in decision-making can improve job satisfaction and reduce frustration with bureaucratic constraints.

5. Addressing Gender Dynamics

The study highlighted significant gender disparities within correctional leadership and a declining number of female staff. Correctional facilities must work to create an inclusive and equitable environment by actively promoting gender diversity in leadership positions and addressing the challenges female officers face in a male-dominated workplace. Initiatives such as gender equity training, mentorship programs for women, and flexible scheduling for work-life balance can help create a more supportive environment for female officers.

6. Encouraging Professionalism and Ethical Conduct

Participants underscored the importance of professionalism, personal integrity, and responsibility in their roles. Correctional facilities should emphasize the value of professionalism through regular training programs that reinforce ethical standards, promote personal accountability, and encourage leadership by example. Recognizing and rewarding officers who demonstrate exemplary professionalism can also enhance morale and motivate others to maintain high standards of conduct.

Summary of the Results

The findings from this study align with previous research on the challenges and motivations of correctional officers, but they also fill an important gap by focusing on the experiences of lead correctional officers. The seven themes identify financial stability, work-life balance, interpersonal relationships, supportive environment, autonomy, professionalism, and gender dynamics—reflect the complex factors influencing job satisfaction and retention in corrections.

By implementing policies that address these motivators, correctional facilities can create a more supportive, inclusive, and fulfilling work environment. These changes improve officers' well-being and contribute to a more effective and resilient workforce, which is essential in the demanding and often stressful environment of corrections.

Conclusions Based on the Results

This study provided valuable insights into what motivates lead correctional officers to remain in their roles. The findings highlight the importance of financial stability, a healthy work-life balance, supportive relationships, and professional growth opportunities in fostering a committed and engaged workforce. Addressing gender disparities and promoting autonomy and professionalism can further enhance job satisfaction.

Correctional facilities prioritizing these factors will be better equipped to retain experienced officers and maintain a stable workforce. By investing in the well-being of their employees, these institutions can improve overall organizational performance and ensure the safety and success of staff and incarcerated individuals.

Comparison of Findings with Theoretical Framework and Previous Literature

The study's findings align with Bandura's (1977) self-efficacy theory, which emphasizes the importance of social support, observational learning, and positive role models in shaping behavior. The presence of experienced, content peers and supportive supervisors provided a model for newer officers, reinforcing their motivation to stay in the field. Additionally, the study's themes of financial stability, work-life balance, and professional growth echo previous research on the factors influencing employee motivation and retention.

Research by Novianty and Evita (2018) on the impact of financial incentives on employee motivation also supports this study's findings, highlighting the importance of competitive compensation and job security in retaining staff. The current study expands on this by exploring how non-financial motivators, such as interpersonal relationships and work-life balance, play a crucial role in job satisfaction.

Interpretation of the Findings

The key findings from this study suggest that a multifaceted approach is needed to address the motivations of lead correctional officers. While financial stability and job security are critical, other factors such as work-life balance, supportive relationships, and opportunities for professional growth are equally important in maintaining a committed and engaged workforce.

Limitations of the Study

This study was limited to lead correctional officers in a midwestern state department of corrections, and the sample size was relatively small. Future research could expand on these findings by including a larger and more diverse sample of correctional officers from various regions and levels of leadership. Additionally, exploring the perspectives of officers who have left the profession could provide further insights into the challenges and motivations associated with retention.

Implications for Practice

The findings from this study have several practical implications for correctional facilities seeking to improve staff retention and job satisfaction. By implementing policies that prioritize financial stability, work-life balance, supportive relationships, professional growth, and gender equity, correctional institutions can create a more engaged and motivated workforce.

Conclusion

In conclusion, the study of lead correctional officers' motivations offers important insights into the factors contributing to job satisfaction and retention in corrections. By addressing the key themes identified—financial stability, work-life balance, interpersonal relationships, supportive environment, autonomy, professionalism, and gender dynamic correctional facilities can foster a more committed and resilient workforce. These findings provide a foundation for future research and practical applications aimed at improving the well-

being and effectiveness of correctional staff.

CHAPTER 6: FUTURE RESEARCH DIRECTIONS

Future studies should expand on the findings of this research by conducting comparative research on lead correctional officers in diverse environments to better understand the external factors influencing their motivation and job satisfaction. Additionally, a deeper exploration of how gender and other diversity factors interact with motivation and well-being could lead to the development of more inclusive and tailored interventions.

Comparative Studies Across Jurisdictions

One of the most promising areas for future research would be to conduct comparative studies of lead correctional officers across different states or countries. Examining how policies, organizational cultures, and correctional systems impact officer motivation could provide valuable insights. For instance, states with differing recruitment practices, benefits structures, or approaches to officer wellness may reveal important variations in job satisfaction and retention. Understanding these variations could help policymakers and correctional administrators identify the best practices contributing to higher motivation and retention across diverse contexts.

Cross-national studies would also offer an interesting perspective, especially in countries with differing correctional philosophies—such as rehabilitation-focused systems versus punitive systems. Investigating the impact of these contrasting approaches on officer motivation and well-being could lead to recommendations for systemic changes that improve outcomes for officers and incarcerated individuals alike.

Gender and Leadership in Correctional Facilities

A significant theme emerging from this research was the gender disparity in correctional facilities, particularly in leadership roles. Participants like P4 and P8 expressed concern about the decline in female staff and the additional challenges women face in male-dominated environments. Addressing this issue is crucial for correctional facilities as they strive to create more inclusive and equitable workplaces.

Future research should explore the barriers that prevent women from entering or advancing within the correctional field. Studies could examine how mentorship, leadership development programs, and gender-inclusive policies influence the career trajectories of female officers. Additionally, understanding the experiences of women who have successfully navigated the challenges of a male-dominated environment could provide valuable insights for creating supportive structures that promote gender diversity in leadership roles.

Intersectionality of Gender and Other Diversity Factors

Another important avenue for future research is the intersectionality of gender and other diversity factors—such as race, ethnicity, and age—on correctional officer motivation and well-being. While this study touched on gender dynamics, future studies could delve deeper into how these intersecting identities influence the experiences of correctional officers.

For example, how do female officers of different racial backgrounds experience the challenges of working in correctional environments? Do officers from minority backgrounds face unique stressors that differ from their peers? Research addressing these questions could lead to the development of more inclusive and targeted interventions that consider the unique challenges faced by a diverse workforce.

Organizational Interventions and Officer Wellness Programs

Future research should also focus on evaluating the effectiveness of organizational interventions to improve officer wellness. Given the findings on work-life balance, stress, and burnout, it would be beneficial to investigate how specific wellness programs—such as mental health support, stress management training, and flexible work schedules—affect job satisfaction and retention.

In addition, longitudinal studies that track the outcomes

of these interventions over time could provide valuable insights into their long-term effectiveness. By identifying which interventions are most effective in reducing stress and promoting well-being, correctional facilities can implement evidence-based strategies tailored to their officers' needs.

Technology and Work-Life Balance

As technology becomes more integrated into various professions, including corrections, future research could explore how technological advancements affect correctional officers' work-life balance. For example, the use of surveillance systems, automated reporting, or even remote working opportunities for administrative tasks could offer solutions for reducing the elevated levels of stress and burnout reported by officers.

Conversely, research should also examine whether the increased use of technology may lead to new stressors, such as constant connectivity or the expectation to remain available outside of normal working hours. Understanding the impact of technology on officer well-being and motivation will be crucial as correctional facilities continue to evolve in the digital age.

Conclusion: A Path Forward

This book sheds light on the often-overlooked experiences of lead correctional officers and provides valuable insights into the factors that motivate them to continue their work in challenging environments. By understanding these motivators, we can work towards creating a more supportive and fulfilling environment for these professionals, who play a crucial role in our justice system.

This qualitative study explored the subjective opinions, attitudes, beliefs, and reflections of lead correctional officers regarding what motivates them to maintain their employment. The research revealed several key factors—such as financial stability, work-life balance, supportive relationships, and professional growth—that contribute to their job satisfaction and retention.

The research also highlighted areas for improvement, such as addressing gender disparities and promoting work-life balance, autonomy, and professionalism. These findings offer a path forward for correctional facilities to implement changes that support their staff, reduce turnover, and improve organizational effectiveness.

Future research can build on these findings by exploring comparative studies, intersectionality, and organizational interventions. By pursuing these avenues, policymakers, correctional administrators, and researchers will better understand correctional officers' motivations and be better equipped to create strategies that enhance job satisfaction, well-being, and performance in the corrections environment.

In summary, this research serves as a foundational step toward improving the working conditions of correctional officers. By continuing to explore their experiences and needs, we can ensure that these essential workers are supported, valued, and equipped to succeed in their roles.

APPENDIX A: DEFINITION OF TERMS

Disciplinary Action:

According to the American Federation of State, County, and Municipal Employees (AFSCME, 2021), disciplinary action includes various corrective measures taken by an employer, such as oral or written reprimands, suspensions (with or without pay), reductions in vacation balance, demotions, or discharges. In cases where disciplinary action is beyond a verbal warning, the employer must provide the employee with written documentation of the action and notify the local union (AFSCME, 2021).

Employee Motivation:

Employee motivation refers to the internal and external factors that stimulate an employee to take action toward achieving specific goals. It includes the direction, intensity, and persistence of behavior, as defined by Pinder (2008). Motivation affects how and why employees engage in their work and can be influenced by rewards, job satisfaction, and personal values.

Intention to Stay:

Shahid (2018) defines intention to stay as the conscious decision made by an employee to continue their employment with a particular organization over a long term. This concept often reflects an employee's commitment and satisfaction with their work environment, role, and organizational culture.

Leadership Hierarchy:

The Minnesota Department of Corrections (2023) outlines a clear leadership hierarchy within correctional facilities, consisting of the following roles:

1. **Trainee Corrections Officer** – Entry-level position for new recruits undergoing training.
2. **Corrections Officer (Sergeant)** – First-line supervisor responsible for overseeing daily operations and ensuring staff and incarcerated individual safety.
3. **Corrections Officer (Lieutenant)** – Mid-level supervisor who manages broader institutional operations and staff performance.
4. **Corrections Officer (Captain)** – Senior supervisory role responsible for overall management and administration within correctional facilities.

Self-Efficacy:

Defined by Bandura (1977), self-efficacy refers to an individual's belief in their capacity to execute behaviors required to produce specific performance outcomes. It influences the approach a person takes to challenges, perseverance, and resilience in the face of difficulties. High self-efficacy often correlates with better performance and job satisfaction.

APPENDIX B: KEY FINDINGS AND CODES

This appendix provides a detailed summary of the key findings from the study, along with the corresponding codes derived from the thematic analysis of interviews with eight lead correctional officers. These codes helped identify patterns and themes that reflect the motivations and experiences of officers in maintaining their employment within the correctional system.

Theme 1: Financial Stability

- **Pattern 1.1: Employment Benefits**
    - **Code 1.1.1**: "I love the amount of time that I get off my vacation."
    - **Code 1.1.2**: "My benefits keep me here; my pension keeps me here."
    - **Code 1.1.3**: "Early retirement and vacation time are huge."
    - **Code 1.1.4**: "I am making good money now as a sergeant."
- **Pattern 1.2: Job Security**
    - **Code 1.2.1**: "I have valuable experience that is useful to people new to the field."
    - **Code 1.2.2**: "I'm too old to start over now."
    - **Code 1.2.3**: "There are a lot of choices and variety within this one field."

Theme 2: Work-Life Balance

- **Pattern 2.1: Stress and Burnout**
    - **Code 2.1.1**: "The stress is off the charts emotionally and physically."

- **Code 2.1.2**: "I need to leave work stress at work and live my life outside of it."
- **Pattern 2.2: Self-Care and Mental Health**
  - **Code 2.2.1**: "Physical exercise helps me decompress."
  - **Code 2.2.2**: "Spending time with my family helps me recharge."
- **Pattern 2.3: Support Systems**
  - **Code 2.3.1**: "I have good people to listen to when I need to talk."
  - **Code 2.3.2**: "Faith plays a big role in helping me through tough times."

Theme 3: Interpersonal Relationships

- **Pattern 3.1: Peer Relationships**
  - **Code 3.1.1**: "We're a tight-knit group; we rely on each other."
  - **Code 3.1.2**: "I enjoy the camaraderie with my colleagues."
- **Pattern 3.2: Supervisor Relationships**
  - **Code 3.2.1**: "Respect and rapport with supervisors are essential for job satisfaction."
  - **Code 3.2.2**: "Some supervisors make coming to work unbearable, while others make it enjoyable."
- **Pattern 3.3: Family Relationships**
  - **Code 3.3.1**: "It's important not to bring work stress home."
  - **Code 3.3.2**: "Working evenings and weekends impacted my marriage."

Theme 4: Supportive Environment

- **Pattern 4.1: Career Advancement Opportunities**
  - **Code 4.1.1**: "There are a lot of career advancement opportunities in the department."
  - **Code 4.1.2**: "I like the idea of moving up through the ranks."

- **Pattern 4.2: Sense of Mattering**
  - **Code 4.2.1**: "I felt that what I was doing mattered, and that gave me purpose."
  - **Code 4.2.2**: "I want to stay because I feel like I'm making a difference."
- **Pattern 4.3: Teamwork and Camaraderie**
  - **Code 4.3.1**: "We are a team; I rely on them, and they rely on me."
  - **Code 4.3.2**: "Being part of a team makes work more bearable, especially in tough situations."
- **Pattern 4.4: Autonomy**
  - **Code 4.4.1**: "I appreciate having autonomy in my decision-making."
  - **Code 4.4.2**: "Leadership positions give me more freedom in my role."
- **Pattern 4.5: Professionalism and Responsibility**
  - **Code 4.5.1**: "I take pride in my integrity and fulfilling my responsibilities."
  - **Code 4.5.2**: "I like helping my team grow and succeed."

Theme 5: Autonomy

- **Pattern 5.1: Desire for Leadership**
  - **Code 5.1.1**: "I enjoy being in charge and leading others."
  - **Code 5.1.2**: "Promotions come with more autonomy, which I value."
- **Pattern 5.2: Frustrations with Organizational Limitations**
  - **Code 5.2.1**: "Micromanagement gets in the way of getting real work done."
  - **Code 5.2.2**: "Sometimes trivial matters are prioritized over important issues."

Theme 6: Professionalism

- **Pattern 6.1: Self-Awareness and Delegation**

- **Code 6.1.1**: "I understand my strengths and weaknesses and delegate tasks accordingly."
- **Code 6.1.2**: "I value finding the right people for the right roles to ensure team success."
- **Pattern 6.2: Work Ethic and Fulfilling Responsibilities**
  - **Code 6.2.1**: "I take pride in doing a good job and helping others."
  - **Code 6.2.2**: "I'm committed to fulfilling my responsibilities, no matter how challenging."

Theme 7: Gender Dynamics in Corrections

- **Pattern 7.1: Decline in Female Staff**
  - **Code 7.1.1**: "The number of female staff has significantly declined over the years."
- **Pattern 7.2: Challenges for Female Officers**
  - **Code 7.2.1**: "It's tough being a female in a male-dominated environment."
  - **Code 7.2.2**: "Working with male incarcerated individuals adds an extra layer of difficulty."
- **Pattern 7.3: Limited Female Representation in Leadership**
  - **Code 7.3.1**: "There are very few women in leadership roles, especially at higher levels."
  - **Code 7.3.2**: "It's hard to advance when there's such limited representation of women in leadership."

This appendix provides a comprehensive view of the codes that helped inform the key findings from this study. Each code corresponds to specific patterns within the seven identified themes, offering a structured understanding of the motivations and experiences of lead correctional officers. These findings are intended to guide further research and inform policies aimed at improving the work environment, retention, and support systems for correctional officers.

REFERENCE

American Federation of State, County, and Municipal Employees. (2021). Agreement between the Minnesota State employees union AFSCME, Council No. 5, AFL-CIO and the State of Minnesota July 1, 2021 through June 30, 2023. https://mn.gov/mmb-stat/000/az/laborrelations/afscme/contract/2021-2023/2021-2023-AFSCME-FINAL-Accessible.pdf

Bandura, A. (1977). Self-efficacy: Toward a unifying theory of behavioral change. Psychological Review, 84(2), 191–215. https://doi.org/10.1037/0033-295X.84.2.191

Bandura, A. (2001). Social cognitive theory: An agentic perspective. Annual Review of Psychology, 52, 1-26. https://doi.org/10.1146/annurev.psych.52.1.1

Burdett, F., Gouliquer, L., & Poulin, C. (2018). Culture of corrections: The experiences of women correctional officers. Feminist Criminology, 13(3), 329-349. https://doi.org/10.1177/1557085118767974

Evers, T. J., Ogloff, J. R. P., Trounson, J. S., &

Pfeifer, J. E. (2020). Well-being interventions for correctional officers in a prison setting: A review and meta-analysis. Criminal Justice and Behavior, 47(1), 3-21. https://doi.org/10.1177/0093854819869975

Fida, R., Laschinger, H. K. S., & Leiter, M. P. (2018). The protective role of self-efficacy against workplace incivility and burnout in nursing: A time-lagged study. Health Care Management Review, 43(1), 21–29. https://doi.org/10.1097/HMR.0000000000000126

Griffin, M. L., Lambert, E. G., Hogan, N. L., Todak, N., & Hepburn, J. (2020). A gendered career stage model to explore turnover intent among correctional officers. The Prison Journal, 100(3), 332–354. https://doi.org/10.1177/0032885520916818

Isenhardt, A., & Hostettler, U. (2020). Incarcerated individual violence and correctional staff burnout: The role of sense of security, gender, and job characteristics. Journal of Interpersonal Violence, 35(1-2), 173-207. https://doi.org/10.1177/0886260516681156

Klinoff, V. A., Van Hasselt, V. B., Black, R. A., Masias, E. V., & Couwels, J. (2018). The assessment of resilience and burnout in correctional officers. Criminal Justice and Behavior, 45(8), 1213-1233. https://doi.org/10.1177/0093854818778719

Kostere, S., & Kostere, K. (2021). The generic qualitative approach to a dissertation in the social sciences: A step by step guide. Routledge. https://doi.org/10.4324/9781003195689

Lambert, E. G., Hogan, N. L., & Griffin, M. L. (2022). Gender differences in how correctional officers experience work-related stress: Implications for support and intervention. Journal of Criminal Justice, 78, 101896. https://doi.org/10.1016/j.jcrimjus.2022.101896

Minnesota Department of Corrections. (2021). 2021 Performance report. https://mn.gov/doc/assets/FY21%20Performance%20Report_Final2_tcm1089-520111.pdf

Minnesota Department of Corrections. (2023b). Job Qualifications. https://mn.gov/doc/employment-opportunities/job-qualifications/

Moon, B., & Maxwell, S. R. (2004). Assessing the correctional orientation of corrections officers in South Korea. International Journal of Offender Therapy and Comparative Criminology, 48(6), 729–743. https://doi.org/10.1177/0306624X04266681

Munger, T., Savage, T., & Panosky, D. M. (2015). When caring for perpetrators becomes a sentence: Recognizing vicarious trauma. Journal of Correctional Health Care, 21(4), 365-374. https://doi.org/10.1177/1078345815599976

Novianty, R. R., & Evita, S. N. (2018). Financial incentives: The impact on employee motivation. Academy of Strategic Management Journal, 17(6), 1-8. https://abacademies.org/articles/financial-incentives-the-impact-on-employee-motivation-7728.html

Office of the Legislative Auditor (OLA). (2020). Safety in State Correctional Facilities: 2020 evaluation report. Minnesota Office of the Legislative Auditor. https://www.auditor.leg.state.mn.us/ped/pedrep/prisonsafety.pdf

Pinder, C. (2008). Work motivation in organizational

behavior. (2nd ed.). Psychology Press.

Rhineberger-Dunn, G., & Mack, K. Y. (2019). Impact of workplace factors on role-related stressors and job stress among community corrections staff. Criminal Justice Policy Review, 30(8), 1204-1228. https://doi.org/10.1177/0887403418787227

Ricciardelli, R. (2017). Canadian provincial correctional officers: Gender strategies of achieving and affirming masculinities. The Journal of Men's Studies, 25(1), 3-24. https://doi.org/10.1177/1060826515624389

Shepherd, B. R., Fritz, C., Hammer, L. B., Guros, F., & Meier, D. (2019). Emotional demands and alcohol use in corrections: A moderated mediation model. Journal of Occupational Health Psychology, 24(4), 438-449. https://doi.org/10.1037/ocp0000114

Trounson, J. S., & Pfeifer, J. E. (2017). Correctional officers and workplace adversity: Identifying interpersonal, cognitive, and behavioral response tendencies. Journal of Correctional Health Care, 23(4), 437–448. https://

doi.org/10.1177/1078345817720923

Van den Broeck, A., Howard, J. L., Van Vaerenbergh, Y., Leroy, H., & Gagné, M. (2021). Beyond intrinsic and extrinsic motivation: A meta-analysis on self-determination theory's multidimensional conceptualization of work motivation. Organizational Psychology Review, 11(3), 240-273. https://doi.org/10.1177/20413866211006173

Vickovic, S. G., & Morrow, W. J. (2020). Examining the influence of work-family conflict on job stress, job satisfaction, and organizational commitment among correctional officers. Criminal Justice Review, 45(1), 5-25. https://doi.org/10.1177/0734016819863099

ABOUT THE AUTHOR

Uyanga Bayandalai, Ph.d

 My passion for this research stems from personal and professional experiences, with a deep desire to contribute to the betterment of correctional facilities and to help leaders within these institutions support and retain their officers. As a corrections therapist and the daughter of a former corrections officer who rose to commissioner in another country, I have a profound connection to this field. Growing up, I witnessed firsthand my father's unwavering dedication to his work, which gave me an early understanding of the profession's profound impact—not only on the officers but their families and communities. This early exposure shaped my career path and fueled my desire to explore the challenges correctional officers face daily. Currently, working in the corrections field myself, I have gained firsthand knowledge of the difficulties and rewards that come with officer turnover and retention. My professional journey includes a Bachelor of Science in Psychology and a Master of Science in Rehabilitation and Addiction Counseling, leading to my current pursuit of a Ph.D. in Psychology. After completing my master's degree, I began working as a clinical program therapist at a Midwestern state corrections facility that provides release and reintegration services. This background has equipped me with a deep understanding of the complexities faced by correctional officers, enabling me to approach this study with both professional insight

and personal sensitivity. In conducting this research, I engaged directly with correctional officers to understand what drives them to remain in such demanding roles. Throughout the process, I was committed to approaching the study with an open mind, ensuring that the voices and experiences of the officers themselves shaped the findings. This work aims to shed light on the experiences of correctional officers and provide actionable insights to inform policies and practices that can enhance their well-being and job satisfaction.

www.ingramcontent.com/pod-product-compliance
Lightning Source LLC
Chambersburg PA
CBHW051653250726
48653CB00007B/2643